Swimming
By the Numbers

Desirée Bussiere

Consulting Editor, Diane Craig, M.A./Reading Specialist

A Division of ABDO

ABDO
Publishing Company

visit us at www.abdopublishing.com

Published by ABDO Publishing Company, a division of ABDO, P.O. Box 398166, Minneapolis, Minnesota 55439. Copyright © 2014 by Abdo Consulting Group, Inc. International copyrights reserved in all countries. No part of this book may be reproduced in any form without written permission from the publisher. SandCastle™ is a trademark and logo of ABDO Publishing Company.

Printed in the United States of America, North Mankato, Minnesota
062013
092013

 PRINTED ON RECYCLED PAPER

Editor: Liz Salzmann
Content Developer: Nancy Tuminelly
Cover and Interior Design and Production: Colleen Dolphin, Mighty Media
Cover Production: Kate Hartman
Photo Credits: Shutterstock

Library of Congress Cataloging-in-Publication Data

Bussiere, Desiree, 1989-
  Swimming by the numbers / Desiree Bussiere.
     pages cm. -- (Sports by the numbers)
  ISBN 978-1-61783-846-0
1. Swimming--Juvenile literature. I. Title.
  GV837.6.B87 2014
  797.2'1--dc23
                        2012049955

SandCastle™ Level: Transitional

SandCastle™ books are created by a team of professional educators, reading specialists, and content developers around five essential components—phonemic awareness, phonics, vocabulary, text comprehension, and fluency—to assist young readers as they develop reading skills and strategies and increase their general knowledge. All books are written, reviewed, and leveled for guided reading, early reading intervention, and Accelerated Reader® programs for use in shared, guided, and independent reading and writing activities to support a balanced approach to literacy instruction. The SandCastle™ series has four levels that correspond to early literacy development. The levels are provided to help teachers and parents select appropriate books for young readers.

Emerging Readers
(no flags)

Beginning Readers
(1 flag)

Transitional Readers
(2 flags)

Fluent Readers
(3 flags)

Contents

Introduction

Numbers are used all the time in swimming.

- Racing pools come in three sizes. Most are 25 or 50 meters long. Some pools in the United States are 25 yards long.

- There are 10 **lanes**. But only 8 lanes are used during a race.

- There are four main swimming strokes. They are freestyle, breaststroke, backstroke, and butterfly.

- There are several races for each stroke. There can be a 100-meter breaststroke and a 200-meter breaststroke.

Let's learn more about how numbers are used in swimming.

The Swimming Pool

82 feet (25 m)

164 feet (50 m)

49 feet (15 m)

16.4 feet (5 m)

The Sport

Swimming **competitions** are called meets.

Swimmers race in groups of 8. Each group is called a heat.

A gun or beep tells the swimmers to start swimming.

A clock measures the time. The fastest swimmer wins.

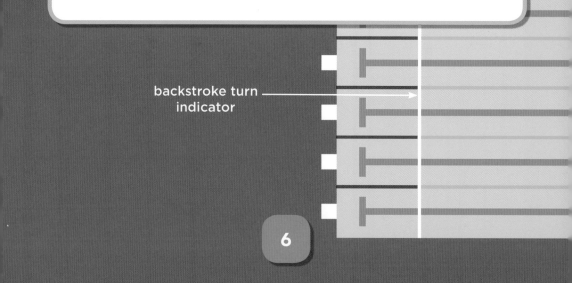

backstroke turn indicator

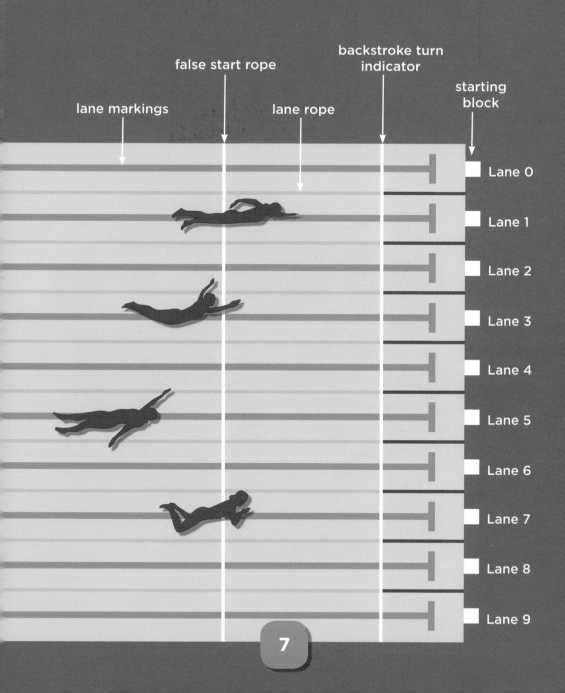

lane markings

false start rope

backstroke turn indicator

lane rope

starting block

Lane 0

Lane 1

Lane 2

Lane 3

Lane 4

Lane 5

Lane 6

Lane 7

Lane 8

Lane 9

Matt is on a swim team.
The team practices early in
the morning.

By the Numbers!

A

Matt's team takes turns swimming **laps** for 1 hour.
Then they use kickboards for 1 hour. How many
hours does the team practice?

(answer on p. 23)

Kyle is a fast swimmer.
He likes swimming
freestyle best.

By the Numbers!

B

Kyle has to swim 6 **laps**. He has finished 4.
How many more laps will he swim?

(answer on p. 23)

Kathy practices starts.
She uses the grab start.

By the Numbers!

C

Kathy did 4 practice starts yesterday. She did 3 starts today. How many total starts did she do?

(answer on p. 23)

Jenna joined the school swim team. She swims the butterfly stroke.

By the Numbers!

D

Jenna swims 4 **laps**. Mark swims 8. How many more laps does Mark swim?

(answer on p. 23)

15

16

Ryan is swimming the breaststroke. The race is 200 meters. It's his favorite event.

By the Numbers!

E

Ryan swam in 7 meets last year. He has been in 2 this year. How many meets has Ryan been in?

(answer on p. 23)

18

Casey is a great swimmer.
She wins a lot of
swimming events.

By the Numbers!

F Casey won 5 **medals** at the meet. She won
2 medals at the last meet. How many more medals
did she win this time?

(answer on p. 23)

Kim swims the backstroke. She watches for the turn **indicator** flags. They tell her she's near the end of the pool.

By the Numbers!

G Kim beat 3 swimmers in the first race. She beat 5 swimmers in the second race. How many total swimmers did she beat?

(answer on p. 23)

Swimming Facts

- Swimming was in the first modern Olympics in 1896.

- The *Titanic* was the first ship to have a heated swimming pool.

- Amy Van Dyken was an American swimmer. She was the first American woman to win 4 gold **medals** at one Olympics.

- Mark Spitz won 9 Olympic gold medals during his **career**.

- After the 2012 Olympics, Michael Phelps had a total of 22 Olympic medals. That is more than any other person in any sport.

Answers to By the Numbers!

A

$$\begin{array}{r} 1 \\ +1 \\ \hline 2 \end{array}$$

Matt's team swims **laps** for 1 hour. Then they use kickboards for 1 hour. How many hours does the team practice?

B

$$\begin{array}{r} 6 \\ -4 \\ \hline 2 \end{array}$$

Kyle has to swim 6 laps. He has finished 4. How many more laps will he swim?

C

$$\begin{array}{r} 4 \\ +3 \\ \hline 7 \end{array}$$

Kathy did 4 practice starts yesterday. She did 3 starts today. How many total starts did she do?

D

$$\begin{array}{r} 8 \\ -4 \\ \hline 4 \end{array}$$

Jenna swims 4 laps. Mark swims 8. How many more laps does Mark swim?

E

$$\begin{array}{r} 7 \\ +2 \\ \hline 9 \end{array}$$

Ryan swam in 7 meets last year. He has been in 2 this year. How many meets has Ryan been in?

F

$$\begin{array}{r} 5 \\ -2 \\ \hline 3 \end{array}$$

Casey won 5 **medals** at the meet. She won 2 medals at the last meet. How many more medals did she win this time?

G

$$\begin{array}{r} 3 \\ +5 \\ \hline 8 \end{array}$$

Kim beat 3 swimmers in the first race. She beat 5 swimmers in the second race. How many total swimmers did she beat?

23

Glossary

career – the work or jobs done over a period of time.

competition – a contest.

indicator – something that is a sign of something else.

lane – a narrow path with something bordering it on both sides.

lap – one time around a track or across a swimming pool and back.

medal – a piece of metal often in the shape of a coin given to the winner of a competition.